Learn to Sell Value

Andrew Howard

Andrew Howard

Copyright Page

Index

Andrew Howard

The Power of Value in Sales

Selling value is much more than just offering a product or service in exchange for money. It is the ability to connect deeply with people's needs and desires, to make them feel that what they are receiving is going to improve their lives in some way. The concept of value in sales refers to the perception that the client has about what they are getting in relation to what they are paying. It is not just about the price, but about the feeling of satisfaction, the resolution of a problem or the achievement of a goal. When someone buys something, they are actually buying a solution, a promise of improvement, and as sellers, our job is to make sure that this promise is not only fulfilled, but that it feels valuable and special.

In the world of traditional sales, price is often thought of as the most important factor. Many salespeople obsess over competing on price, lowering rates or offering discounts to attract more customers. However, what truly distinguishes a successful sale is the customer's perception of value. The customer will be willing to pay more for something if they feel that something is really worth it, if they believe they are getting more than they pay for. And that's the trick: our job is not to compete on price, but on value.

Imagine you walk into a store looking for a new phone. In the first store you are shown the cheapest model, told that it is functional and does the basics. In the second store, the salesperson explains how that same model fits your needs, shows you features you may not have known existed, tells you how you can use the camera to improve your vacation photos, and offers personalized customer service if you ever have a problem. Both phones cost the same, but in the second store, you feel like you are getting more. The perceived value is greater, even though the price is identical. This is the power of value in sales.

Adding value is not just about offering something extra, but doing it in a way that makes the customer feel important, relevant and personal. Often, small details can make a big difference. A follow-up call after a purchase to make sure everything is going well, a personalized recommendation, or even simply explaining in a clear and detailed way how the product works, are gestures that can transform the shopping experience. These details not only reinforce the idea that something of quality is being offered, but they also build a relationship of trust between the seller and the customer.

Furthermore, value is not only measured in functional terms. There are emotional and psychological elements that play a fundamental role in how the customer perceives a purchase. Trust in the brand or the seller, the feeling of exclusivity or personalization, good treatment and the overall shopping experience are factors that add value. If a customer feels listened to, understood and valued, they will be more willing to make the purchase, and most importantly, they will feel that what they are acquiring is much more valuable.

The real challenge of selling value is doing it from the right approach. If we only try to sell a product without thinking about the customer's needs, we will probably lose opportunities. But if our mission as sellers is to thoroughly understand what the person is really looking for, and from there we show them how our product or service can improve their life, we are creating a much stronger and longer-lasting relationship. At that moment, the sale stops being a transaction and becomes genuine help.

The power of value in sales is also in how we position ourselves as problem solvers, not just salespeople. When someone comes to us looking for something, what they are really looking for is an answer to a need or a desire. If we can show them that what we offer not only meets that need, but does so more efficiently, more conveniently, or more satisfactorily than other options, then we are creating real value. At that point, the customer's perception of value increases, and with it, their willingness to buy.

So it's not about competing on who can offer the lowest price, but on who can offer the most value. People are always willing to pay more if they feel they're getting something that's really worth it. And that something can be tangible, like better quality, or intangible, like the peace of mind that comes from knowing they're in good hands. Whatever we offer, we need to make sure the customer sees, feels and understands that they're getting more than just a product, that they're getting value.

Ultimately, selling value is a philosophy. It is a way of doing business where the focus is not on closing the sale at any cost, but on making sure the customer leaves the interaction feeling like they have gained something meaningful. It is a long-term strategy, because a customer who perceives value is a returning, recommending, and trusting customer. And that trust is what turns an occasional sale into a lifelong relationship.

The First Step to Adding Value

Adding value in a sale is not something that happens by chance. It is the result of careful planning and, above all, a deep understanding of who you are selling to. The first step to being able to offer value is to know the customer – and I don't just mean knowing their name or what they need at that moment, but really understanding them as a person. This means that you must go beyond the surface and make an effort to know their concerns, their desires, what frustrates them and what motivates them. The better you know them, the easier it will be to identify how you can add value to their life.

To start, it's important to remember that every customer is unique. Several people may be interested in the same product, but that doesn't mean they're all looking for it for the same reasons. Some people may be motivated by quality, others by price, and others by the experience they'll get from using the product. If you can figure out what really drives your customer, you can tailor your approach and offer them something that they really care about. This is where value comes in, because it's not just about what you sell, it's about how you make them feel. And to do that, you need to know them well.

The key to knowing your customer is research and observation. Before you try to sell something, ask yourself: what is this person really looking for? What problem do they have that they need solved? These questions are essential because they will help you see beyond the transaction. If you can understand the customer's problem or need from their point of view, you will be in a much better position to offer a solution that will truly add value to them. This also means that you need to be a very good listener. Listening is one of the most important skills in sales, but it's not enough to just hear what they say – you also need to understand the context behind their words. Sometimes customers don't directly express what they need, but if you pay attention, you will be able to identify those signals.

A common mistake in sales is assuming that all customers are looking for the same thing or that their motivations are obvious. For example, a person who walks into a store looking for a laptop may be motivated by a variety of reasons: maybe they need something quick for work, maybe they're looking for a tool to study with, or maybe they just want something that will let them watch movies and browse the internet. If you try to sell them the most expensive computer just because you think that will get you a bigger commission, you're likely to lose the sale. However, if you take the time to get to know their needs, you can figure out what they're really looking for and offer them the best option to meet those needs, which will ultimately add much more value to the purchase.

Knowing your customer also means knowing their current situation and potential constraints. Some people may have budget constraints, others may be looking for something that saves them time, while others are interested in a product that makes their life easier. If you can understand those constraints, you can tailor your offer to better fit what they are looking for. This is where you can really make a difference, because successful selling is not just about offering what you have, but offering what the customer needs in a personalized way. This is where you start to generate real value.

It's also important to recognize that value isn't always measured in terms of money. Sometimes, a customer may be willing to pay more for something if they feel you're offering them something valuable, such as an extended warranty, additional technical support, or exceptional customer service. These factors don't have to do directly with the product, but they do affect how the customer perceives the value of what they're buying. So, knowing your customer allows you to figure out what additional aspects you can add to the shopping experience to make them perceive greater value.

Another key aspect of getting to know your customer is understanding their emotions. Buying decisions are influenced by emotions as much as logic. If a customer trusts you, if they feel that you understand them and care about what they are looking for, they will be much more likely to perceive greater value in what you offer. Sometimes, just taking the time to ask questions and listen can be enough to make a customer feel that you are valuing them as a person, not just as another sale. That feeling is invaluable, and it is one of the most effective ways to add value.

In addition to listening, it's also essential to observe. Pay attention to how the customer reacts to what you're showing them. If they seem hesitant or unsure, perhaps they need more information or a better explanation of how your product can meet their needs. If they're excited or seem interested in a specific aspect, focus on that and explain how that particular detail can be beneficial to them. Close observation will help you adjust your approach in real time, which will increase the likelihood that the customer will perceive value in what you're offering.

Finally, it's important to remember that customer insight isn't a process that's completed in one go. It's something you need to cultivate over time. The more you interact with your customers, the more you'll learn about them, and that information will allow you to continue to adjust and improve the way you add value. Plus, when a customer feels understood and valued, they'll not only be more likely to buy now, but they're also likely to return in the future and recommend you to others.

In short, the first step to adding value in a sale is to know your customer deeply. This knowledge allows you to offer customized solutions, adapt your approach, and build trust. It's not just about selling a product, but about solving problems and improving people's lives in a meaningful way. When you truly know your customer, you can add value in ways that others can't, and that's the key to building long-lasting, successful relationships.

Listen to Understand, Not to Sell

Listening is a skill that, although it seems simple, is often overlooked in the world of sales. Many salespeople focus so much on what they want to say or how to present their product that they forget something fundamental: what the customer is really saying. But there is a big difference between simply hearing what someone says and truly understanding them. Listening to understand is a much deeper approach, and it can completely change the outcome of a sale. It's not about waiting your turn to speak, or thinking about how to close the sale while the customer explains their situation. It's about paying genuine attention and understanding what the person needs, feels and is looking for.

When we talk about listening to understand, we mean putting our full attention on the customer, without distractions or hidden agendas. Instead of focusing on what you are going to say next or on the quick answer to convince the customer, your attention should be fully on what the customer is telling you. Not just on the words they use, but on the tone of voice, the emotions they show and the gestures they accompany their speech.

People do not always say exactly what they want or need, but if you really listen to them, you can pick up much more than they are willing to reveal with words. This is a key aspect of adding value: understanding the customer's true motivations in order to offer them an appropriate solution.

One of the most common mistakes salespeople make is interrupting a customer before they finish speaking. Sometimes, it's easy to be tempted to want to correct them, give a quick answer, or assume what they're going to say before they finish explaining it. Not only can these types of interruptions frustrate the customer, but they also cause you to miss out on valuable information. If you interrupt, you're depriving yourself of understanding the full picture. Listening attentively not only shows respect, but it allows you to pick up on important details that you might miss if you're too focused on selling.

Listening to understand also means asking questions to clarify what you don't understand or what you need to dig deeper into. Don't be afraid to ask for more details or ask additional questions. These questions shouldn't be asked with the goal of pushing the customer toward a purchase, but rather to better understand their situation, needs, and concerns. For example, if a customer mentions that they need a time-saving solution for their business, you could ask them, "What are the specific tasks that take up the most time in your day-to-day life?" Not only do these types of questions show genuine interest in their problem, but they allow you to identify how your product or service can be a customized solution for that specific need.

Another key aspect of listening to understand is to avoid assumptions. Sometimes we think we already know what the customer wants because we've heard something similar before, or because we think our product is the perfect solution to every problem. But every customer is different, and their needs, even if they seem similar, can be unique. If you assume you already know the answer before the customer finishes speaking, you could offer them something that isn't what they really need. The only way to ensure you're offering the right value is to listen with an open mind, without jumping to conclusions.

Listening also has a direct impact on trust. When a customer feels like you are listening to them, and that you really care about what they have to say, they are more likely to trust you. Trust is one of the fundamental pillars in any successful sales relationship. No matter how good your product or service is, if the customer doesn't trust you, they will hardly feel comfortable making a purchase. By listening to understand, you are showing the customer that their satisfaction is your priority, not just closing the sale. Not only does this help close the sale at that moment, but it can also build a long-term relationship, as customers value salespeople who truly care about their needs.

Furthermore, listening gives you a strategic advantage. By fully understanding what the customer is looking for, you can tailor your offer or presentation much more effectively. For example, if you know that the customer has a particular concern, such as product durability, you can focus on that aspect and show how your product excels in that field. Or if the customer is more concerned about technical support, you can highlight the warranties and after-sales services you offer. This way, your offer becomes much more personalized and relevant to the customer, which increases the perception of value.

Another benefit of careful listening is that it helps you anticipate objections. Customers often indirectly express their concerns or doubts about a product or service while discussing their needs. If you're paying attention, you can spot those points and address them before they become formal objections. For example, if a customer mentions that they've had bad experiences with similar products in the past, you can use that information to explain why your product is different and how they can avoid those problems. This allows you to not only offer an appropriate solution, but also alleviate any concerns the customer may have.

Listening to understand also requires patience. Sometimes, customers need time to explain what they're really looking for. They may not express it clearly from the start, or they may need to explore several ideas before reaching a conclusion. As a salesperson, your job is to give them that space, allow them to speak without rushing, and make sure they feel comfortable sharing their thoughts. Patience is a virtue in sales, and when customers feel like you're not rushing them, they're more likely to open up and share more important details about what they really need.

At the end of the day, listening to understand, not to sell, is one of the most powerful strategies you can use to add value. It allows you to connect with the customer on a much deeper level, helps you offer personalized and relevant solutions, and builds trust and loyalty. Salespeople who master this skill not only close more sales, but they also build stronger, longer-lasting relationships with their customers. And when customers feel like you really understand them, that's when they start to see the true value in what you offer them.

How to Position Your Product as a Valuable Solution

Positioning your product as a valuable solution is essential to making customers perceive it as something they actually need in their lives. It's not enough to simply show what your product or service does, you have to get people to see it as the answer to a problem they face or as a significant improvement in their lives. The key is to shift the conversation from what your product offers to what it can do for the customer. It's about creating a connection between the product's features and the customer's needs. When you get the customer to see the real value they can get, they're more likely to be willing to make the purchase.

To start, it's critical to understand that people don't buy products, they buy solutions. This means they aren't interested in the technical details or feature list of what you're selling unless those features have a direct impact on their life. For example, if you're selling a car, the customer isn't as interested in the horsepower or engine size; what they care about is how that car can improve their daily experience, whether it will save them time, whether it's safe for their family, or whether it will provide comfort on their commute. You need to be able to translate your product's features into tangible benefits that the customer can value.

One of the first things you need to do to position your product as a valuable solution is to understand the problem the customer is trying to solve. This involves listening carefully and asking key questions that help you identify their needs. If you know exactly what the customer's problem is, you can show them how your product fits their specific situation. For example, if you sell a time management app and you find that your customer is having trouble organizing their workday, you can explain how your app will help them increase their productivity and reduce stress, rather than just talking about the software's features.

Another important aspect is to highlight the unique benefits of your product. Your product will almost always have competition, so you need to make it clear what makes it different and, most importantly, why that difference is valuable to the customer. It's not just about being better overall, but about being better at what's most important to your customer. If your product has a special feature that solves a common problem more effectively than other products on the market, that's something you need to highlight clearly and directly. By doing so, you're helping the customer understand that your product isn't just another option, but the best option for their specific needs.

It's also crucial to tell stories that connect emotionally with the customer. Stories have the power to make the value of your product feel more real and accessible. You can tell examples of how other people have used your product and how it has improved their life or business. These stories allow the customer to imagine themselves using the product and getting the same benefits. For example, if you sell accounting software and tell the customer how a small business owner like them managed to simplify their finances and save time thanks to the software, the customer is likely to relate and see the real value they can get. Stories create an emotional connection that reinforces the perception of value.

Additionally, you must be able to clearly communicate the return on investment

(ROI) that the customer will get from using your product. This does not necessarily mean a financial return, although in some cases it can. ROI can be measured in time saved, convenience, personal satisfaction, stress reduction, or any other benefit that is important to the customer. When you can get the customer to see that the investment they are making in your product will return something much greater than what they are paying, the perceived value increases considerably. If you sell a web design service, for example, you could explain how an investment in a professional website will attract more clients and generate more sales, which will translate into profits far greater than the initial cost.

Another key point is to make the customer feel that your product is designed specifically for them. This can be achieved by personalizing your message and adapting your presentation to each customer's particular needs. If you make the customer feel that your product is tailor-made to solve their unique problem, this will automatically increase the perception of value. For example, if you sell technology solutions, instead of offering a standard package, you could suggest a customized approach based on the specific needs of the customer's company. This customization not only makes them see that your product is suitable for their situation, but also reinforces the idea that you are interested in helping them find the best solution.

Trust also plays a huge role in the perception of value. To position your product as a valuable solution, you need to make sure that the customer trusts what you are offering. Trust is built with honesty, transparency, and support. Make sure you clearly explain what your product can and cannot do, and don't make over-the-top promises that you can't keep. Customer testimonials, case studies, and satisfaction guarantees are effective ways to build trust. If the customer knows that others have already had good results with your product and that you are confident enough to offer a guarantee, they are more likely to perceive your product as valuable.

Another aspect to consider is the shopping experience. It's not just about the product itself, but also how the customer feels throughout the buying process. A smooth, hassle-free shopping experience accompanied by excellent customer service can significantly increase the perception of value. If the customer feels that you are taking care of them from the very first moment, that you offer support, that you answer their questions and that you are there to help them at every step, their perception of your product will be much more positive.

Finally, always remember that perceived value is subjective. You can't force a customer to see your product as valuable, but you can guide them to discover the value for themselves. This is achieved through clear, honest communication that focuses on the benefits that really matter to the customer. When you get the customer to see how your product improves their life, solves their problems, or provides them with something meaningful, you have positioned your product as a valuable solution. And when a customer perceives value in something, they will be willing to invest in it without hesitation.

Adding Emotional Value

Adding emotional value to a product or service is one of the most powerful ways to connect with customers and get them to perceive something far beyond the tangible. Emotions play a crucial role in the decision-making process, and when you get a customer to feel emotionally attached to what you offer, you are creating value that cannot be measured in economic terms alone. People don't always buy because they need a product; they often buy because that product makes them feel something, whether it's happiness, pride, security, or even connection. This type of emotional value is what transforms a simple transaction into a meaningful experience, and it's what can differentiate your product or service from any other on the market.

One of the first steps to adding emotional value is to understand that emotions are what drive many purchasing decisions. When a person buys a product, they are not just purchasing an object or a service, they are purchasing an experience. For example, when someone buys a car, they are not just purchasing a means of transportation. They may be purchasing the feeling of freedom that the car offers them, the security they feel knowing they are protecting their family, or even the status that comes with driving a specific model. In the same way, when someone buys a perfume, they are not just purchasing a fragrance, but the confidence they feel when wearing it and the emotion it provokes in others. The product itself is only one part of the total value; the emotion it generates is what really matters.

To achieve this, it is essential to create a story around your product or service that connects emotionally with customers. Stories are a powerful tool because they appeal directly to human emotions. If you can tell the story of how your product was created, why it is important, or how it has changed the lives of others, you will be adding an emotional level that will resonate with people. For example, if you sell eco-friendly products, you can tell the story of how those products are helping to protect the environment and care for the planet for future generations. This story will touch the emotions of those who value sustainability and want to feel good about their purchasing decisions, knowing that they are contributing to a greater cause.

Additionally, adding emotional value involves making the customer feel special and appreciated. People want to feel valued, and when you make a customer feel like they are more than just a number or a transaction, a stronger emotional connection is created. This can be achieved through small details, such as personalized service, a sincere thank you after a purchase, or post-sale follow-up that shows you care about their satisfaction. These gestures are not necessarily expensive or difficult to implement, but they have a profound impact on how the customer perceives the relationship with your brand. When a customer feels that you truly value them, their loyalty to your product or service increases considerably.

Another important aspect is that emotional value can also be added through the experiences you offer alongside your product or service. Experiences can be even more memorable than the product itself. For example, a technology company that offers innovative products can also organize exclusive events for its customers where they are allowed to try out new releases before anyone else. This not only creates a sense of exclusivity but also generates excitement and enthusiasm around the brand. These emotional experiences reinforce the bond between the customer and the product, making the purchase much more than just a transaction; it becomes a memorable event.

Authenticity also plays a key role in creating emotional value. Customers are increasingly adept at spotting when a company or salesperson isn't authentic, and this can turn people away rather than attract them. To add true emotional value, you need to be genuine in your approach. If you talk about the positive impact of your product on people's lives, make sure those claims are real and verifiable. If you promise a particular emotional experience, such as well-being, satisfaction, or happiness, you need to deliver on that promise. Authenticity builds trust, and trust is a powerful emotion that can influence long-term purchasing decisions.

Personalization is another key element when it comes to adding emotional value. People like to feel unique, and when you can tailor your product or service to feel personalized, the emotional value is significantly increased. It's not just about embossing the customer's name on a product, but making the entire experience feel tailored specifically for them. This could be through personalized recommendations based on their preferences, or offering products that solve their specific problems. When a customer feels like you've paid attention to their individual needs and are offering them something that's made for them, their emotional connection to what you offer will be much stronger.

It's also important to remember that adding emotional value doesn't always mean creating immediate positive feelings. Sometimes emotional value is created by helping a customer overcome a difficulty or face a challenge. For example, if your product or service helps people overcome a difficult situation, such as a health problem or a stressful moment in their lives, you'll be creating lasting emotional value. This type of emotional connection can be even stronger, as people look back with gratitude on times when someone or something helped them improve their situation. If you can make your product associated with solving an important problem, the perception of emotional value will be immense.

Customer loyalty is another great outcome of emotional value. People don't always remember the exact details of what they bought, but they do remember how they felt during the purchasing process and how the product made them feel afterward. If your product or service manages to generate positive emotions, customers are more likely to buy from you again and recommend you to others. Emotions are contagious, and a satisfied customer who has experienced a strong emotional connection with your brand will talk about it with their friends, family, or colleagues. Not only does this increase the perception of value for them, but it also extends that emotional value to other potential customers.

Finally, don't forget that adding emotional value is an ongoing process. It's not just about creating a positive emotion during the purchase and then forgetting about the customer. You need to keep nurturing that emotional connection over time, through exceptional customer service, constant communication, and offering new experiences that keep the emotion they felt at the beginning alive. Brands that manage to maintain this emotional connection over time are those that build long-term relationships with their customers, and those relationships are the foundation of a successful business.

In short, adding emotional value is a key strategy to differentiate your product or service in a competitive market. It's about creating a connection beyond the functional, making customers feel something that motivates them to choose your brand over others. When you manage to touch the right emotions, you're not just selling a product, you're creating an experience that customers will value and remember.

Andrew Howard

The Art of Educating the Customer

Educating the customer is one of the most important skills you can develop when looking to add value in the sales process. It's not just about selling the customer something, but making sure they fully understand what they're buying, how they can benefit from it, and why your product or service is the best option to solve their needs. Educating the customer means patiently and clearly guiding them through the buying process, giving them the information they need to make an informed decision. When the customer feels educated and not just sold to, their trust in you and what you offer grows considerably. And when there's trust, sales become more fluid.

The first thing you need to understand is that most people don't always know what they need or how a product can help them. Sometimes, they aren't even aware of the problem they have until someone explains it to them. That's why educating the customer starts by helping them understand what their current situation is and how your product or service can make their life easier, more comfortable, or more efficient. This means that you need to be more than a salesperson; you need to become a guide, someone who accompanies the customer in the process of discovering what they really need. This approach will not only help you close more sales, but it will also position you as an authority in your field.

A key aspect of customer education is to avoid the temptation to just talk about your product. If you focus solely on the features of what you're selling without explaining how these features help the customer, you risk losing their interest. Instead, you should take the time to show them how those features solve a problem or improve their life in some way. If you're selling a vacuum cleaner, for example, the customer doesn't need to know that it has a high-powered motor or that it weighs five kilos. What they really care about is that the vacuum cleaner can clean their house in half the time and that it's easy to operate. The key is to translate technical information into practical, easy-to-understand benefits.

Patience is a very valuable tool when educating a customer. It's common for customers to not fully understand a product or service right off the bat, and it's your job to take the time to explain things clearly. Sometimes, it can be frustrating to have to repeat the same thing over and over again, but if you do it patiently and kindly, the customer will appreciate it. Not only will this make them feel more comfortable with you, but it will also build a relationship of trust. Customers tend to value more those salespeople who take the time to explain everything clearly, without rushing or pressuring them. Remember that a successful sale is not about rushing the customer, but about making sure that they truly understand the value of what they are buying.

It's also important to remember that educating the customer doesn't end when the sale is made. In fact, real education often begins after the customer has purchased your product or service. You need to make sure they know how to use it properly to maximize the benefits. This is particularly important when it comes to more complex products or services. A well-educated customer is much more likely to be satisfied with their purchase, which means they're more likely to return for future purchases and recommend your product or service to others. You could even offer tutorials or guides that explain how to get the most out of their purchase, to ensure their experience is as positive as possible.

A key part of educating your customer is being transparent. Customers want to know exactly what they're getting and how the product or service works. If you try to hide details or make promises you can't keep, you'll not only lose the sale, but also the customer's trust. You need to be honest about your product's capabilities and limitations. If a customer has a question about something that isn't clear, answer truthfully, even if the answer isn't what they were hoping to hear. This honesty not only builds trust, but it also reinforces your image as a trustworthy seller who truly wants the best for their customers.

Additionally, it's important to tailor your educational approach to the customer's level of knowledge. Some customers will already know a lot about the type of product or service you offer, while others will have no idea where to start. You need to be able to adjust your pitch based on the customer's level of knowledge so as not to overwhelm them with unnecessary information or bore them with details they already know. If a customer is already well-informed, focus on the details that could make the difference for them. If, on the other hand, they are new to the topic, start with the basics and gradually increase the complexity of the information. This way, you ensure that each customer receives the amount of information they really need.

An effective technique for educating customers is to use concrete examples. People learn best when they can visualize how a product or service can tangibly impact their lives. You can use examples of other customers who have had similar problems and how your product or service helped them solve those problems. This form of teaching is much more powerful than simply listing features, because it allows the customer to see how what you offer can be directly applied to their situation. For example, if you sell project management software, you could tell the story of how a small company was able to increase their productivity and reduce the chaos in their day-to-day life thanks to your software. Concrete examples allow the customer to imagine using the product and seeing the results in their own life.

One interesting aspect of educating your customer is that often times, what you teach isn't directly related to your product, but it's still valuable to the customer. For example, if you sell financial consulting services, you can educate the customer on good financial habits in general, not just how to use your services. This type of additional education shows that you care about their well-being beyond the sale, and that strengthens your relationship with the customer. Plus, when you offer free and useful educational value, the customer is more likely to view you as a valuable resource and trust you when it comes time to purchase.

Another powerful tool to educate customers is to leverage online content. Nowadays, many customers prefer to do their own research before making a purchasing decision. If you can offer educational resources on your website, such as blogs, videos, or tutorials, you'll be helping customers learn for themselves while also positioning yourself as an authority on the topic. These resources not only educate, but they also keep customers interested in what you offer, creating a constant connection with your brand. Plus, by educating the customer online, you can reach more people efficiently and effectively.

Lastly, don't forget that customer education is an ongoing process. It's not something that happens overnight, but rather requires time and dedication. Customers are likely to have questions or concerns over time, and being available to them is crucial. When a customer feels like they can count on you for answers and guidance at any time, their trust in you and your product will grow. Ongoing education creates lasting relationships, and those relationships are what will lead to long-term success.

In short, the art of educating a customer is about helping them understand how your product or service can improve their lives, providing them with the information they need in a clear and accessible way, and accompanying them throughout the entire purchasing process and beyond. When you successfully educate a customer, you are not only facilitating a sale, but you are building a relationship based on trust and value, which is essential for success in any business.

The Philosophy of Helping First, Selling Later

The "help first, sell later" philosophy completely changes the traditional way of looking at sales. For a long time, sales have focused on closing the deal as quickly as possible, on persuading the customer to buy regardless of whether what they are acquiring is really what they need. But in a world where customers are increasingly informed and demanding, that mentality no longer works the same way. Today, consumers are looking for more than just a transaction; they want to feel that they are making an intelligent decision, that they are really receiving value, and that the person or company selling to them cares about their interests. This is the essence of the help first, sell later philosophy: it is about putting the customer's needs first, offering solutions before offering products, and building a relationship based on trust.

The traditional sales approach often creates a kind of natural distrust in customers. We have all been in situations where we feel that a salesperson is only interested in their commission or in selling us something quickly, regardless of whether we really need it or not. In these cases, we feel pressured, uncomfortable, and often decide not to buy simply because we don't want to fall into that trap. On the other hand, when the approach is based on helping first, the customer feels more relaxed, valued and, most importantly, understood. This opens the door to a much more honest and fluid conversation, where the customer can express their true concerns and where you, as a salesperson, have the opportunity to offer an appropriate solution.

The idea of helping first means that you shouldn't immediately focus on the product or service you're selling, but rather on the customer's needs and problems. It's important to listen carefully to what the customer is saying, ask questions that dig deeper into their concerns, and look for solutions that truly add value to them. This may mean, in some cases, that the product you're selling isn't the best option for them at that moment, and that's okay. The simple act of recommending something that's more suitable, even if it's not what you're selling directly, can build a long-term relationship of trust. People value those who help them without a hidden agenda, and this keeps them coming back again and again when they need something in the future.

A clear example of this philosophy can be seen in businesses that focus on customer service. Imagine walking into a store looking for a solution to a specific problem. If the salesperson immediately tries to convince you to buy the most expensive product or the one that generates the most profit, you are likely to feel distrustful. But if that same salesperson takes the time to understand what you really need and recommends something that not only solves your problem but also fits your budget and expectations, you will feel grateful and trusting. This type of interaction not only leads to an immediate sale, but also builds a long-term relationship. The next time you need something, you will probably return to that same store because you will remember how they helped you without putting pressure on you.

Another important aspect of this philosophy is that by helping first, you are positioning yourself as a trusted advisor, not just a salesperson. People tend to be loyal to those who give them good advice and help them make informed decisions. When customers perceive that your primary goal is to help them, they are more willing to listen to what you have to say and trust your recommendations. This way, you become not just someone who sells products, but a trusted source they will turn to whenever they need to solve a problem or make an important purchasing decision.

A common misconception is that helping first means not selling. In fact, it's quite the opposite. A help-first philosophy increases the chances of closing a sale because customers, feeling cared for and understood, will be more willing to buy something that solves a real problem for them. Instead of feeling like they're being manipulated, they feel like they're making a decision based on the information you've provided them. This decision is much more solid and satisfying, leading not only to a sale at that moment, but also to future purchases, referrals, and loyalty to your business.

Helping first also means anticipating your customer's needs. This means you should know your product or service well, but also the context in which your customer is going to use it. You should be able to foresee what problems they might face and offer solutions before they even realize they need them. This kind of anticipation reinforces the idea that you are there to help, not just sell. For example, if you work in software sales and you know your customer is purchasing a tool to improve their team management, you could offer additional advice on how to implement it correctly, or suggest a technical support package to ensure everything runs smoothly. This proactive help not only adds value to the product, but also shows that you really care about your customer's success.

It's important to note that helping first doesn't always mean offering solutions that involve a direct sale. Sometimes, the best way to help a customer is to provide valuable information, even if it doesn't lead to an immediate purchase. This can be guidance, advice, or simply taking the time to answer their questions without expecting anything in return. This type of interaction builds trust and creates a long-term relationship with the customer. When the person is ready to buy, they'll remember that you were the one who helped them, and they'll be more inclined to buy from you.

There is also an emotional component to this philosophy. Humans are emotional creatures, and our purchasing decisions are often influenced by how we feel. When a customer feels like they are being sincerely helped, that their interests are being prioritized, and that they are receiving real value, they are much more likely to experience positive emotions associated with the purchase. These emotions can include gratitude, trust, confidence, and satisfaction. These are all emotions that increase the likelihood of a sale and, most importantly, a lasting relationship between customer and salesperson.

In this help-first philosophy, the focus is on building relationships, not just making a sale. Long-term relationships are far more valuable than quick sales. A customer who trusts you will not just buy from you once, but will come back when they need something else, and will even recommend you to other people. This is far more cost-effective in the long run than focusing on immediate sales. Also, loyal customers tend to be less price-sensitive, as they value the quality of service and the trust you've built with them more. In other words, the help-first philosophy creates customers who not only buy, but also become ambassadors for your brand.

In short, the help-first, sell-later philosophy is a strategy that can transform the way you do business. It's about putting the customer's needs first, building relationships based on trust, and offering value before you even talk about a sale. It's an approach that not only increases the odds of closing sales, but also creates loyal customers who will be willing to come back again and again. When you help first, you're investing in long-term relationships that are far more valuable and lasting than any quick sale. This is the true value of selling with a helper mentality.

How to Create Memorable Experiences

Creating memorable experiences for your customers is one of the most powerful strategies you can use to stand out in a competitive market. Nowadays, customers are not just looking for products or services; they also want to experience something unique, something that makes them remember the purchase as more than just a transaction. Creating memorable experiences is, in essence, turning the act of selling into something that goes beyond the simple exchange of money. It is about connecting with the customer's emotions, surprising them, and providing them with an experience that not only meets their expectations, but exceeds them. When you achieve this, your customer will not only be satisfied, but will become an ambassador for your brand, someone who will talk about you enthusiastically and recommend what you offer.

One of the keys to creating a memorable experience is paying attention to the small details. Often, it's not the product itself that makes a customer remember a purchase, but the way they were treated or how they felt during the process. For example, if a customer walks into a store and is greeted with a genuine smile, a pleasant atmosphere, and friendly service, that first impression is already creating a positive experience. Those small details, which may seem insignificant, are what make all the difference. It doesn't cost anything to be kind or attentive, but the impact it has on the customer is huge.

In addition to the small details, it's important to create surprise moments. We all like to receive something unexpected, something we didn't see coming. This doesn't mean you have to give away things or make grand gestures all the time, but think about how you can surprise your customers in creative ways. It can be something as simple as a handwritten thank you note after a purchase, or an unexpected discount on their next purchase. It can also be offering them an extra service they weren't expecting, such as helping them solve a problem that isn't directly related to what you sell, but that improves their overall experience. These surprise moments make a big impression on customers because they aren't used to receiving more than they paid for. When they do, that feeling of gratitude and surprise stays with them long after the purchase.

Another important aspect of creating memorable experiences is personalizing your customer interaction. No one likes to feel like just another number on a list or a generic shopper. When you make your customer feel like they are special, that you know them and care about their specific needs, you are giving them an experience they can't find anywhere else. A good example of this is remembering the names of your regular customers, knowing what they frequently buy, or being attentive to their preferences. In the digital world, this can be done through personalized emails or product recommendations based on previous purchases. But, even in a face-to-face interaction, small gestures like asking about their preferences or remembering personal details can make a big difference. Personalizing your treatment makes the customer feel valued and gives them the feeling that you really care about their well-being, not just their money.

The shopping experience doesn't end when the customer pays and leaves. A common mistake many businesses make is thinking that once the money has changed hands, the job is done. In reality, the most important part of creating a memorable experience can happen after the purchase. Post-sale follow-up is a great opportunity to show the customer that you care about their long-term satisfaction. You can send them an email or make a call to make sure they're happy with what they bought, or ask if they have any questions or concerns. This type of after-sale care can make a huge difference in how the customer perceives their overall experience. Even if they had a problem or issue, your willingness to resolve it quickly and efficiently can transform a negative situation into a memorable experience.

The environment in which the customer interacts with your business also plays a key role in creating a memorable experience. If you have a physical store, you need to think about all the aspects that affect the customer's experience when they walk in. The décor, music, lighting, aroma, and the order in which the products are arranged are all factors that influence how the customer feels while in your store. For example, a welcoming and well-designed environment can make the customer feel comfortable and relaxed, which improves their willingness to buy. If you have an online business, the user experience on your website is just as important. The site should be easy to navigate, aesthetically pleasing, and fast in its response times. A simple and efficient checkout process makes the customer feel well cared for and valued.

Communication is also a key element in creating a memorable experience. From the first contact with the customer, whether in person, on the phone or via email, the way you communicate will set the tone for the experience they will have. You should be clear, friendly and always available to resolve questions or concerns. Open, fluid communication builds trust, and trust is an essential component of creating a memorable experience. If the customer feels that they can talk to you without problems, that you are always available to help and that you are interested in what they have to say, they are much more likely to have a good impression of their interaction with you.

It's important to note that not all memorable experiences have to be tied to a huge effort or investment of considerable resources. Often, the most memorable experiences are those that demonstrate genuine care for the customer. Listening to what they have to say, showing empathy for their situation, and being willing to go the extra mile to make their life easier are simple but powerful ways to create an emotional connection with the customer. For example, if a customer has a problem with a product and you resolve it quickly, without putting up roadblocks, they will not only be satisfied, but will remember that positive experience every time they think of your business.

One of the great benefits of creating memorable experiences is that you're not only increasing the likelihood that the customer will return, but you're also creating a story that the customer will want to share with others. In the marketing world, this is known as "word of mouth marketing," and it's one of the most effective ways to attract new customers. When a customer has such a good experience that they feel the need to tell their friends, family, or social media about it, they're doing the work of promoting your business for you. And the best part is that this type of promotion is completely genuine. There's no better advertising than a sincere recommendation from someone who's had an amazing experience with your brand.

Finally, to create memorable experiences, you must be willing to continually adapt and improve. Customer expectations change over time, and what was memorable in the past may not be so in the future. That's why it's crucial to always be on the lookout for customer feedback, learn from their experiences, and look for ways to improve what you offer. Listening to feedback and adjusting your approach will not only help you continue to wow your customers, but it will also keep you one step ahead of the competition.

In conclusion, creating memorable experiences is one of the best ways to differentiate yourself and build a strong relationship with your customers. This isn't about spending a lot of money or making grand gestures, but about paying attention to details, surprising the customer with small actions that show you care, personalizing the treatment and making sure the shopping experience is smooth and enjoyable. When you get a customer to leave with a smile, you've created an experience they'll remember and share, which will not only increase their chances of coming back, but also attract others. Creating memorable experiences is a long-term investment that yields great rewards in terms of loyalty and growth.

How to Increase the Value of Your Product or Service

Increasing the value of your product or service is one of the most important strategies to stand out in the market and ensure that customers choose what you offer over the competition. Often, value is not just in what the product is, but in how it is perceived, in the experience surrounding the purchase, and in what it means to the customer. Value, then, is not limited to the cost or features of the product; it extends to everything the customer receives before, during, and after the purchase. When you manage to increase the value of your product or service, you can not only justify a higher price, but you can also generate stronger loyalty in your customers, because they will feel truly satisfied with what they get.

One of the first steps to increasing the value of your product or service is to improve the customer's perception of what you offer. This means that you need to make sure that the customer clearly understands all the benefits that they will receive by purchasing your product. Often, sellers focus only on the product's features, as if the customer can automatically interpret how those features will be useful to them. But that's not always the case. A customer needs you to explain clearly and directly how those features translate into solutions to their problems or needs. For example, if you're selling a mobile phone, it's not enough to say that it has a long-lasting battery or a high-quality camera; you need to explain how those features will make their life easier or improve their daily experience, whether by allowing them to take high-quality photos at any time or by saving them from having to constantly charge their phone.

Another effective way to increase the value of your product or service is to add additional benefits that are not necessarily related to the product itself, but that complement the customer experience. These additional benefits can be after-sales services, extended warranties, free technical support, or access to exclusive resources. A clear example of this is when you buy an electronic device and, in addition to getting the product, you are offered a free installation service or a 24/7 customer support line. These additional benefits are not a direct part of the product, but they increase its value by offering the customer something more than just the item they purchased. These additions make the customer feel like they are getting more for their money and that they are really making a smart purchase.

Service quality is also a key factor in perceived value. Even if your product is great, if your customer service is poor, the perceived value will decrease considerably. Customers don't just buy products; they buy experiences. If they feel well cared for, listened to, and valued from the start, they will view your product or service in a more positive light. Good customer service includes prompt responses, friendly treatment, and the ability to resolve problems efficiently. Additionally, if you can personalize the service in some way, such as remembering the names of frequent customers or their preferences, you will be creating a stronger connection that will increase the perceived value of what you offer.

Another important strategy to increase the value of your product or service is to create a narrative around it. People love stories, and when you can associate your product with a compelling story, its value automatically increases. It's not just about what you sell, but "why" you sell it. For example, if you have a company that makes clothes, you can tell the story behind how you select materials, how you make sure workers are treated fairly, and how each garment is produced sustainably to protect the environment. Suddenly, the product is not just a piece of clothing; it is a garment with a purpose, with a positive impact. This adds an emotional and ethical value that many customers are willing to pay for. By humanizing your product through a story, you make it more valuable because the customer connects not only with the item, but also with the values and principles behind it.

In addition to telling a compelling story, exclusivity can play a big role in value perception. People tend to value more what is exclusive or limited, as they feel like they are getting something that not everyone can have. This doesn't mean you should artificially limit the availability of your product, but you can find ways to make it feel special. For example, you could launch limited editions, offer customized products, or give early access to certain customers. These strategies make the customer feel like they are getting something unique, which increases their perception of value.

The shopping experience is also a critical factor in value perception. Make sure the experience is smooth, pleasant, and hassle-free. If you have a physical store, pay attention to the environment: make sure it is welcoming, well-lit, and organized. If you sell online, make sure the website is easy to navigate, the checkout process is quick, and the customer receives clear and detailed confirmations. The simpler and more pleasant the experience, the more value the customer will perceive. No one wants to go through a frustrating purchase, even if the product is great. A bad experience can significantly reduce the perceived value of the product, while a pleasant shopping experience can increase it, even if the product is the same.

Another way to increase the value of your product or service is to offer additional training or advice. In many cases, the customer may not be entirely sure how to use the product to its fullest, or may have questions about how to get the best results. If you can offer tutorials, user guides, or even personalized advice, you'll be adding value by helping them get the most out of their purchase. For example, if you sell software, you could offer free training for customers to learn how to use all the features. This type of support not only improves customer satisfaction, but also increases perceived value, as the customer feels like they're getting much more than just a product.

Community is also a powerful way to add value. If you can create a community around your product or service, where customers can interact with each other, share tips, or learn from each other, you have created additional value that goes beyond what you offer. Many successful companies have accomplished this by creating forums, social media groups, or events exclusive to their customers. When customers feel like they are part of a community, they are not just purchasing a product, but are participating in a collective experience that enriches their lives. This sense of belonging adds value in a way that few other strategies can achieve.

Finally, the perception of value is also increased when the customer feels they are getting a fair deal. This doesn't necessarily mean you should lower your prices, but you should make sure the customer clearly understands why your product or service is priced the way it is. Transparency is key here. Explain clearly why the price is fair, highlighting the costs associated with the quality of the materials, the effort behind the manufacturing process, or the benefits your service offers. When customers understand the "why" behind the price, they are more willing to pay because they feel they are getting commensurate value.

In short, increasing the value of your product or service goes far beyond improving its features. It's about improving customer perception, adding extra benefits, providing excellent service, telling a compelling story, offering a pleasant shopping experience, providing additional support, building a community, and being transparent about pricing. All of this contributes to the customer feeling like they're getting much more than just a product; they're getting a complete experience that justifies the price and, more importantly, makes them feel satisfied and valued. When you achieve this, you're not just selling a product or service; you're creating a long-term relationship with your customers, who will see in your offer a value that goes beyond the tangible.

Selling Value Instead of Price

Selling value instead of price is one of the most important strategies for any seller who wants to stand out in today's market. Often times, when customers compare products or services, the first thing they look at is price. This can lead to aggressive competition based solely on who offers the lowest price. However, that is not a sustainable or effective strategy in the long run. Constantly cutting prices can erode profits and, in some cases, cause the product or service to lose quality. Additionally, competing on price alone does not create a strong connection with the customer. Instead, selling based on the value you offer can transform the way customers view what you sell, leading to a longer-lasting and more rewarding relationship.

When we talk about selling value, we mean making the customer understand that what they are buying goes far beyond the monetary cost. It is not just the product or service that matters, but the total experience, the additional benefits, the long-term satisfaction and the solution you are providing. When you manage to sell with this mindset, the price becomes a secondary factor, because the customer understands that they are getting something of much more value than what they will pay. This is where the concept of value becomes so powerful: while price is a number, value is a feeling, a perception of how much something can improve the customer's life.

The first step to selling value instead of price is to change your approach as a seller. If your mindset is focused on competing for the lowest price, you'll be sending the message that the product is only worth what it costs. But if you focus on highlighting the benefits, advantages, and difference your product or service can make in the customer's life, you'll be selling much more than a financial transaction. You'll be selling a solution, an experience, a transformation. To achieve this, you need to know very well not only what you sell, but also the deep needs of your customer. What problems do they have? How can your product improve their life? What worries them or what do they look for in a solution? When you understand this, you can position your offer as something valuable, beyond just the number on the label.

A key aspect of selling value is to focus on the results the customer will get. It's not enough to talk about the technical features or details of the product; what the customer really wants to know is how that product or service will change their life or business. If you sell software, for example, instead of focusing only on the features it has, you should talk about how that software will save time, reduce errors, and improve efficiency in daily work. If you sell clothing, it's not just the fabric or the design that matters, but how it will make the customer feel when wearing it, what impression it will make in a meeting, or how it will make them look more confident. By highlighting the results the customer will get, you're showing the true value of your product or service, and price becomes a much less relevant issue.

Additionally, selling value also involves educating the customer. Often times, customers are not fully informed about everything your product or service can do for them. As a salesperson, it is your responsibility to make sure they understand all the benefits and advantages they will gain. This doesn't mean bombarding them with information, but rather guiding them in a clear and simple way toward understanding how your offering is the best option for them. When customers are well-informed, they tend to make decisions based more on value than price. For example, if a customer is considering two products and one of them is more expensive, but you are able to clearly explain why your product offers more value in terms of durability, performance, or additional service, they are more likely to choose your offering, even if it is priced higher.

Another important aspect of selling value instead of price is creating a memorable shopping experience. From the first moment a customer comes into contact with your brand, they should feel like they are getting something special. This can be through exceptional customer service, a simple and personalized checkout process, or even small details that make the experience more enjoyable and meaningful. When a customer feels like they are being treated specially, they automatically perceive more value in what they are buying. It's the difference between going to a store where the staff treats you impersonally and one where they greet you by name, offer recommendations based on your previous preferences, and make you feel like someone valuable. That kind of experience adds value that goes far beyond the product itself.

It's also important to note that selling value doesn't mean you have to ignore price altogether. You can actually use price as a way to reinforce value. If you have a product that's more expensive than your competition, instead of apologizing for the price, you can use it as an opportunity to explain why it costs more. A higher price can be a signal of quality, exclusivity, or additional benefits that your competition doesn't offer. The key is for the customer to understand exactly why they're paying more and what they'll get in return. If you can communicate this effectively, the customer will see the price as an investment, not an expense.

Plus, when you sell value instead of price, you're building long-term relationships with your customers. By focusing on what really matters to them, you're showing them that you're not just interested in making a quick sale, but that you genuinely want to help them improve their lives or solve their problems. This mindset builds trust and loyalty, and when a customer trusts you, they're willing to keep buying, regardless of the price. A loyal customer isn't just looking for the best price; they're looking for the best experience and the best long-term value. This is how you keep them coming back again and again, because they know they're getting much more than just a product from you.

One of the great advantages of selling value is that it takes you away from price wars. Competing on price alone is a race to the bottom, where in the end no one wins, neither the seller nor the customer. When you sell value, you can justify higher prices, maintain your margins, and most importantly, create a clear differentiation from the competition. While others worry about lowering prices, you focus on increasing customer-perceived value, which puts you in a stronger position and allows you to build a more loyal and satisfied customer base.

Finally, selling value also means making sure the customer has a good post-purchase experience. It's not enough to make a good sale; you need to make sure the customer continues to perceive value even after they've paid. This can be through excellent after-sales service, personalized follow-up, or even small gestures like thanking them for their purchase or offering them additional recommendations based on their preferences. When a customer feels they continue to receive value after the purchase, they're more likely to come back and recommend your product or service to others.

In short, selling value instead of price is a strategy that not only helps you stand out in a competitive market, but also allows you to build stronger, longer-lasting relationships with your customers. It's about focusing your efforts on what really matters to the customer, showing them how your product or service can improve their lives, and creating a shopping experience that goes beyond price. When you manage to do this effectively, price becomes secondary and the customer will be willing to pay more, because they know that what they are receiving has a much higher value.

Andrew Howard

How to Change Customer Perception of Value

Changing a customer's perception of the value of a product or service is a task that requires a conscious and strategic approach. The way a customer perceives the value of what you're offering them isn't always aligned with reality. Sometimes, a customer may view a product as expensive, unnecessary, or of lower quality simply because they don't fully understand its benefits or because they're comparing it to cheaper alternatives. As a salesperson, your job is to help the customer see beyond the price or initial appearances, and show them that what you're offering is actually worth it. Changing that perception doesn't happen overnight, but with the right tools, it's possible to transform how customers value what you sell.

The first step to changing a customer's perception of value is to understand how that customer currently views your product or service. This means that you have to make an effort to listen to and understand their expectations, concerns, and needs. If the customer perceives the product as expensive, why does he think that? Is he comparing it to a cheaper option? Does he not understand all the benefits your product offers? Knowing exactly how the customer is thinking gives you an important advantage because you can focus your efforts on the areas where the perception is most wrong. Here, dialogue with the customer becomes fundamental, since only by asking and exploring what they really think will you be able to detect the barriers to their perception.

Once you understand current perceptions, the next step is to educate the customer about the true value of your product or service. Education is one of the most powerful tools for changing perceptions, as many times the customer is simply not aware of all the positive aspects your product can offer. To educate effectively, it is not enough to just give a list of technical features or a bunch of data that the customer may not understand or appreciate. What really works is showing how your product can solve a specific problem or improve their life in a tangible way. You must be able to clearly and simply communicate why your product is the best option for the customer, how it can benefit them, and what differentiates it from other options on the market.

It's important to remember that humans make purchasing decisions not only with their heads, but also with their hearts. This means that changing the perception of a product's value is not only about logic and data, but also about emotions. To change the perception of value, it's key to make the customer feel emotionally connected to what you offer. For example, if you sell a car, don't just talk about the engine power or the mileage. Instead, talk about the experiences the customer will have with that car, how safe it will be to travel with their family, or how proud they will be to drive it. Emotions are a very powerful lever to change perception, and when you get the customer to feel an emotional connection to your product, they are much more likely to perceive greater value in it.

Another way to change a customer's perception of value is through testimonials or success stories. Sometimes a customer doesn't fully trust what you're telling them until they see real examples of people who have already used your product or service and had positive results. Testimonials are a great way to show value in action. When a potential customer sees that others have achieved real results, solutions, or benefits from your product, their perception immediately changes. Success stories also work because they allow the customer to imagine themselves in that same successful situation. Instead of just seeing themselves buying a product, they see themselves enjoying the benefits that the product offers them, which reinforces the perception of value.

Additionally, to change the customer's perception of value, you need to make sure you create a positive buying experience from the first contact. If the customer has a negative experience, either because the purchasing process is complicated, the customer service is not adequate, or they simply do not feel taken care of, the perception of value will be affected from the start. On the contrary, when the customer feels that the entire purchasing process is fluid, pleasant and well taken care of, they automatically tend to perceive more value in the product or service. It is important to remember that you are not just selling a product; you are selling an entire experience. The way you treat the customer and how you make them feel throughout the process can drastically influence how they perceive what you offer.

Another key aspect of changing the perception of value is offering additional benefits that they weren't expecting. This can be something as simple as good after-sales service, an extended warranty, or even a small gift with the purchase. These unexpected details help create a feeling that the customer is getting more than they pay for, which immediately changes their perception of value. It's not just what they're buying, but everything that comes with that purchase. These types of actions reinforce the idea that what you offer is not only worth what it costs, but even exceeds expectations. And when you exceed expectations, the customer walks away with a much higher perception of the value of your product or service.

On a psychological level, it is also important to play with the concept of scarcity and exclusivity to change the perception of value. When a product is perceived as scarce or exclusive, the customer tends to value it more. This is something that occurs naturally in human behavior: what is harder to get or what is exclusive automatically seems to have more value. If you can position your product or service as something unique or limited, the customer is much more likely to see it as something of greater value. This does not mean that you should falsify information, but you can emphasize unique aspects of your product that make it more attractive and valuable.

Another way to influence customer perception of value is by using strategic comparisons. Often, a customer needs a point of reference to understand why something is worth what it is. If you can make a clear comparison between your product and the competition, showing why what you offer is superior, you can help change perception. However, it is important that these comparisons are honest and focus on what really makes the difference. It is not about badmouthing the competition, but rather highlighting what makes your product a better investment for the customer.

Finally, to change a customer's perception of value, you need to be patient and consistent in your messaging. Changing a perception doesn't happen immediately; it can take time, especially if the customer already has a preconceived notion or has had bad experiences in the past. The key is to keep communication clear, consistent, and focused on the benefits that really matter to the customer. If you manage to maintain that focus and are consistent in showing how your product or service offers real, tangible value, eventually the customer will start to see things differently. It's an investment of time, but the results are worth it.

In short, changing customer perceptions of value is a process that requires education, emotions, concrete examples, and a positive experience. By understanding how the customer currently views your product, educating them on the real benefits, connecting with them emotionally, and offering them an experience that exceeds their expectations, you can transform the way they value what you offer. Not only will this help you close more sales, but it will also allow you to create stronger, longer-lasting relationships with your customers, based on a mutual understanding of the true value you provide.

Andrew Howard

Building Long-Term Relationships Based on Value

Building long-term relationships based on value is one of the most important aspects for any business that wants to thrive sustainably. Selling a product or service just once is not enough to guarantee long-term success. What really matters is how you can keep your customers happy, satisfied and convinced that they will always receive something of value from you, beyond the initial transaction. Value-based relationships not only allow customers to come back again and again, but they also promote loyalty, positive word of mouth and a solid reputation. To achieve this, it is essential to understand that it is not just about selling, but about cultivating a genuine relationship with your customers, based on trust, respect and, above all, on the value that you constantly offer them.

The first step to building long-lasting relationships is to be authentic from the start. Customers know when a salesperson is being sincere or just interested in closing a sale. If you show a genuine intention from the start to help the customer, listen to them, and solve their problems, that relationship will start on a solid foundation. This authenticity is key to making the customer feel like they can trust you. You don't want to promise things you can't deliver or exaggerate the benefits of your product. If the customer perceives that you are deceiving or manipulating them, the relationship will quickly break down. Therefore, being honest and transparent at all times is the foundation on which long-term relationships are built.

Another essential aspect is showing your customers that you value them, not just as a buyer, but as a person who trusts your product or service. To do this, you need to invest time and effort into getting to know your customers more deeply. This means actively listening to what they say, understanding their needs and problems, and offering solutions that really help them. The more you understand your customers, the easier it will be for you to add value to their lives, as you can tailor your products or services to what they really need. This personalization not only shows them that you care about their experience, but it also reinforces the idea that you are committed to helping them, which is essential to maintaining a long-term relationship.

Building value-based relationships also means continuing to provide support even after the sale has been made. Many businesses make the mistake of forgetting about the customer once the transaction has been completed. However, true value is demonstrated when, after the sale, you remain available to answer questions, offer assistance, or provide additional recommendations. This type of after-sales service is crucial to demonstrate that your relationship with the customer does not end when payment is received, but continues over time. When a customer sees that you are willing to stay in touch and provide ongoing support, they feel much more valued and are more likely to purchase again in the future.

A key component to strengthening a long-term relationship is consistently exceeding customer expectations. When you manage to surprise your customer with something they didn't expect, such as an added benefit, extra service, or simply personalized attention, you are adding more value than they initially expected. This "added value" doesn't have to be something big or expensive. It can be a small detail, such as a personalized thank you note, a special discount for being a repeat customer, or even a personalized follow-up to make sure the product they purchased is meeting their expectations. These details show that you care about their satisfaction and are willing to go the extra mile for them.

Another important factor in building value-based relationships is consistency. A customer needs to know that they can trust you every time. This means that every time you interact with them, they should receive the same level of quality in product, service, and attention. Inconsistency breeds distrust and can ruin the relationship. If you provide excellent service one time and the customer has a mediocre experience the next, their perception of value will be negatively affected. On the contrary, if you always deliver what you promise and make sure that every interaction is positive, you will be creating a solid foundation for a long-lasting relationship.

Regular communication is also key to keeping the relationship alive. It's not about bombarding the customer with offers or advertising messages, but rather keeping them informed about news relevant to them, asking them about their experience or simply being available when they need you. This constant, but balanced communication reinforces the idea that you care and are always willing to help. Also, by keeping an open channel of communication, you can identify any problems that may arise and solve them before they negatively affect the relationship. Feedback is also essential. Asking your customers about how to improve your products or services not only helps you improve, but also shows them that you value their opinion.

One aspect that can't be ignored is reciprocity. When you focus on giving value first, rather than asking for something in return, you create a bond of trust. Customers who feel like they've received more than they expected, without feeling pressure to buy, tend to develop a deeper, more genuine relationship with the company. This philosophy of giving before receiving reinforces the idea that you care more about helping them than simply making a sale. Over time, this reciprocity builds loyalty, as customers value companies that truly care about their well-being more.

Furthermore, building long-term value-based relationships requires adapting to changing customer needs. People change, their needs evolve, and what brings value to them today may not do so in a year. That's why it's essential to always be aware of how those needs are changing and adjust your products or services accordingly. If you manage to stay relevant to the customer, anticipating their future needs, you will become a trusted resource that they will seek out on a recurring basis. This not only strengthens the relationship, but also ensures that your offer continues to be seen as valuable over time.

Innovation plays an important role here. You can't expect to maintain a long-term relationship if you always offer the same thing without improving or evolving. Customers appreciate it when a company keeps up to date, looks for ways to improve, and offers new solutions. This doesn't mean you should radically change what you offer, but it is important to be open to new ideas, updates, and continuous improvements that add value to the customer experience.

Finally, it is important to remember that building long-term value-based relationships is not a quick process. It requires time, dedication, and patience. Customers will not become loyal overnight, but if you constantly work on offering them value, listening to their needs, surprising them with additional details, and maintaining open and honest communication, you will be building a relationship that will not only allow you to retain those customers, but will also make them recommend you to others. Value-based relationships are the best strategy for a successful and sustainable business in the long term, because they are not based solely on the transaction, but on the positive impact you generate in the lives of your customers.

Making Value Your Company's Culture

Making value your company culture is an approach that transforms the way you do business—not just for immediate success, but for long-term growth. When we talk about making value a core part of your company culture, we're talking about much more than just delivering a good product or service. We're talking about building a company that, in every aspect of its operation, from how it treats employees to how it engages with customers, is geared toward delivering something valuable, authentic, and meaningful. Not only does this approach have the power to differentiate you from the competition, it also creates a solid foundation of trust and loyalty that can take your company to the next level.

The first step to making value an integral part of your company culture is to start from within. If employees don't believe in the value they're providing, or if they don't understand what it means to add value, it will be difficult to convey that to customers. That's why it's essential that everyone in the company, from management to the sales team, share the same vision of what it means to create value. This can be achieved through clear communication and ongoing training, where all employees understand the importance of being customer-centric and how to add value in every interaction. If every team member is aligned with this vision, the company culture will begin to reflect that commitment to value.

Making value your company culture also means establishing clear values that guide all decisions. These values should be more than just words on a wall or in an employee handbook; they should be principles that guide the behavior of every person in the company. For example, if one of your values is honesty, then all interactions with customers should be transparent, with no over-promising or underhanded tactics. If respect is a core value, that should be reflected in how you treat customers and employees, both in person and in communications. These values form the heart of a value culture, and when applied consistently, they help establish a strong foundation on which to build lasting customer relationships.

Another important aspect of creating a value-centric culture is a focus on continuous innovation. Value is not static;

it must constantly evolve as customer needs and expectations change. Companies that succeed in making value part of their culture are those that are always looking for new ways to improve their products, services, and customer experience. This doesn't mean you should always reinvent the wheel, but it does mean having an open mindset to change and being willing to adapt your offering to stay relevant. When a company commits to innovating for the benefit of its customers, it shows that it is dedicated to providing real long-term value, not just selling something once.

Additionally, making value your company culture means always putting the customer at the center of all decisions. This means that every time you make an important decision, whether it's about launching a new product, changing prices, or the way you serve customers, you should consider how that will impact the value you're providing. If customers feel that they are always being considered and that their needs are a priority, a relationship of trust will be established. This customer orientation should also be reflected in the way complaints or problems are handled.

Companies that have made value their culture see customer problems as opportunities to improve and strengthen the relationship, not as obstacles.

How the company is led is also crucial to fostering a value culture. Leaders must lead by example, demonstrating in their daily actions how that value is lived. If company leaders are not committed to adding value or do not behave in accordance with the stated values, it will be difficult for employees to do so. Leadership that truly embodies value principles creates an environment where employees are motivated to do the same. Leaders must be committed to providing support, resources, and guidance, not only for the team to sell more, but to better understand how to provide lasting value to customers.

Making value your company culture also involves recognizing and rewarding employees who really excel at adding value. This can be as simple as public recognition at a team meeting or a more formal incentive. The point is, when employees see that their effort to add value is appreciated, they will be more motivated to continue doing so. Creating a culture of value isn't something that can be achieved from the top alone; it needs to be something that everyone in the company embraces and promotes, and that requires efforts to be recognized and celebrated.

Another key aspect is maintaining a strong relationship with your company's suppliers and collaborators. If suppliers see that they are also treated with respect and that value is sought in the relationship, they will be more willing to collaborate to improve the final offer to customers. Strong, value-based relationships with suppliers can help you obtain better products, services, and prices, which at the end of the day also translates into more value for your customers. This focus on value should be part of all the relationships that the company maintains, not only those that it has directly with customers.

It's important to remember that creating a value culture takes time and effort. It's not something that happens overnight, and it's not something that can be implemented superficially. For it to really work, it needs to be deeply embedded in the way the company operates, at every level. From internal policies to the way products are developed and customers are interacted with, value must be the guiding principle that guides all actions. This requires a firm commitment and a clear vision of what you want to achieve.

It is also important that the value culture does not become stagnant. As the market evolves and customers change, the company must be willing to adjust its approach to continue to provide relevant value. This may mean keeping an eye on new market trends, constantly listening to customer feedback, and being willing to change when necessary. Maintaining flexibility and openness to change is essential to ensure that the value culture remains effective and that the company continues to be seen as a trusted source of value for its customers.

Ultimately, when you make value your company culture, you create an environment where everyone benefits: customers, employees, and the business itself. Customers experience real, lasting value, which keeps them coming back again and again. Employees feel motivated because they know they're working for something that truly matters and that makes people's lives better. And business thrives because a culture of value builds loyalty, trust, and a positive reputation that's hard to beat. Not only does this approach help you sell more, it positions you as a company that's committed to making a difference in the lives of its customers—which, at the end of the day, is the real key to success.

www.ingramcontent.com/pod-product-compliance
Lightning Source LLC
Chambersburg PA
CBHW051857130726
47987CB00002B/867